MPN voice

www.mpnvoice.org.uk

Copyright © 2022 MPN Voice

DISCLAIMER

MPN Voice has used its best efforts in preparing this recipe book from community submissions. MPN Voice makes no representation or warranties with respect to the accuracy, applicability, fitness, or completeness of the contents of this book. The information contained within is strictly for educational purposes. Therefore, if you wish to apply ideas contained within this book you are taking full responsibility for your actions.

MPN Voice is not a licensed medical authority and is not providing medical advice or diagnosing or treating any condition you may have. Always consult with your healthcare team about your personal health, medical and inflammatory related issues. The contents of this book is presented for information purposes only and is not intended as medical advice, nor to replace the advice of a medical doctor or other healthcare professional. Anyone wishing to embark on any dietary, exercise or lifestyle change for the purpose of preventing or treating a disease or health condition should first consult with, and seek clearance and guidance from, a competent healthcare professional.

The information within this book should not be construed as specific advice. It is presented for the sole purpose of stimulating awareness of healthy eating that may help the reader achieve better health.

Any individual wishing to apply the information within this book for the purposes of improving their own health should not do so without first consulting with a qualified medical practitioner. All patients need to be treated in an individual manner by their personal healthcare team.

The decision to utilize any information within this book is ultimately at the sole discretion of the reader, who assumes full responsibility for any and all consequences arising from such a decision. The authors and MPN Voice shall remain free of any fault, liability or responsibility for any loss or harm, whether real or perceived, resulting from the use of information within this book.

Special thanks to: Guy's & St Thomas's Foundation, Debbie Street and all the contributors, without who, this book would not exist.
Designed by: Mark Taylor

MPN Voice
Guy's & St Thomas' Foundation
The Grain House, 46 Loman Street, London, SE1 0EH
Registered Charity Number: 1160316
Company limited by guarantee registered in England & Wales No. 9341980
Email: info@mpnvoice.org.uk

A Poem by Bernadette Dillon-Ryan

Flick through the pages. Come - take a look.
At this deliciously new MPN book.

With recipes to browse you'll be eager to try it -
The anti-inflammatory 'Mediterranean diet '.

Concoctions with vegetables
And lush vibrant fruits
Wholegrains and fish -
So many dishes to choose!

Drizzle with olive oil
As you take a sip of some wine.
Smell the aromas emerged,
Once all has combined

And some benefits you will see
With this simplest of ways -
The Mediterranean diet
To help your MPN days.

Contents

Foreword

Thank you for opening this book - the brainchild of Alice a patient whom you will meet on the adjacent page, and whilst inspired by the MPN patient, clinical and scientific community, the book reflects the collective effort of Alice, her family and the MPN Voice team.

MPN …. What's that? As a blood cancer consultant for over 20 years specialising in MPN, or myeloproliferative neoplasms, I would tell you these are rare blood cancers affecting around 15,000 people in the UK at the present time. MPN can be diagnosed at any age, my youngest patient is two years old and my oldest just over a hundred. All may have abnormal blood counts, some have large spleens, itchy skin, debilitating fatigue, blood clots in unusual places and an early death; whilst others have no symptoms or complications. Yet all MPN sufferers face the difficulty of having a disease most people haven't heard of, where few can be cured (due to the substantial risks of a bone marrow transplant) and where predicting the future can be difficult.

Inflammation is a hallmark of MPN and important in several ways. We recently learnt that the very beginnings of an MPN can been detected decades before a diagnosis is made with a very small number of blood cancer cells, it is thought that inflammation is important in driving over time the increase in number of MPN cells, and indeed other cancer cells leading to the development of disease. Inflammation is also linked to MPN symptoms such as fatigue and finally to increased risk of thrombosis or blood clotting events such as heart attack or stroke. Indeed, the benefits of an anti-inflammatory diet extend to reducing the risk of these events for people who do not have an MPN and are subject to investigation in the MPN field by the international community including a dear friend and long-term colleague Professor Ruben Mesa who has also contributed to these pages.

This book contains a collection of recipes from Alice, fellow MPN patients and their families as well as more information about MPN, tips for living well and information about the charity, MPN Voice, launched by myself and a group of wonderful patients more than a decade ago. The MPN Voice mission is to provide clear and accurate information and emotional support to everyone who has been diagnosed with MPN and their families and friends. The charity vision and desire is that one day there will be a cure and an answer to what causes MPN.

I have known Alice for over 7 years now, she is an MPN patient, an extraordinary, inspirational young woman and indeed a doctor herself having recently been awarded a doctorate degree. Thank you for supporting Alice, MPN Voice and the MPN community by purchasing this book. Enjoy the recipes and explore the benefits of the anti-inflammatory diet in the process making a potential investment in your own well-being and supporting the mission of MPN Voice.

Professor Claire Harrison

The idea for this recipe book came from members of the MPN Voice community who had firsthand experience of the benefits a healthy, Mediterranean, anti-inflammatory diet can bring. Symptoms can have a significant impact on patients' lives and the chronic nature of MPNs means it can sometimes feel as though there is little we can do to control what's happening inside of us. Managing the food that we eat is just one way of taking ownership over our diseases and potentially improving our quality of life.

This is particularly important given exciting new research which suggests a healthy diet, comprising of anti-inflammatory foods and ingredients, could have a positive impact on MPNs. Dr Angela Fleischman at the University of California Irvine has begun to study the relationship between nutrition and MPNs, and early results suggest a healthy, Mediterranean-style diet could be extremely beneficial. Her research builds on existing knowledge about the positive impact a Mediterranean diet can have in patients with cardiovascular diseases which, like MPNs, are characterised by chronic inflammation. Fleischman's hypothesis is that inflammatory cytokines are likely to be involved in producing MPN symptoms and driving disease progression. Reducing these inflammatory markers through a healthy, Mediterranean diet therefore has the potential to relieve symptoms and change future disease trajectories.

This book, then, seeks to build on Fleischman's work and the positive testimonies of our patients and bring the community together in a shared conversation about nutrition and MPNs.

It is important to acknowledge that changing your diet takes time and energy. It can be difficult to plan homecooked meals if you're working and don't have a helping hand in the kitchen. The price of food in the cost-of-living crisis also poses a challenge to buying healthy or organic ingredients which are sometimes costlier than processed foods and 'ready meals' lauded in supermarket offers. Similarly, it's not straightforward or realistic to cut out *all* inflammatory foods and ingredients. But things are changing. Plant-based alternatives are increasingly popular and environmental consciousness is persuading us to eat local and reduce our meat intake. It is often said, "every little helps", and even a small step towards a Mediterranean-style diet could make a big and lasting difference.

This is a special recipe book curated by the MPN community *for* the MPN community. Thank you to everyone who submitted their favourite recipes which fill these pages. We hope it will help raise awareness about nutrition, inflammation and MPNs, and spark more conversations about the steps we can take to improve our health and wellbeing. To our knowledge, it is the first of its kind in the MPN community and represents an important step forward in creating more self-help resources for patients in the UK and worldwide. By purchasing this book, you will be making a valuable contribution to MPN Voice and its vital work in supporting the patient community.

We'd like to end by wishing you "bon appetit" as you embark on your next culinary adventure...

Alice, aged 27, with JAK2+ ET

About MPN Voice

MPN Voice's mission is to provide clear and accurate information and emotional support to everyone who has been diagnosed with a myeloproliferative neoplasm (MPN) and their families and friends.

The volunteers who founded MPN Voice (previously known as MPD Support Charity and MPD Voice), wanted to provide a source of professionally backed information, build and facilitate an MPN community and advocate for patients affected by this rare group of blood cancers.

MPN Voice is still run by volunteers comprising MPN patients and healthcare professionals who continue to share this vision.

Over the years MPN Voice has developed to provide a wide range of unbiased and medically backed information including leaflets, newsletters, regional and online forums where MPN patients can meet and hear about the latest MPN research.

MPN Voice has also invested in research, supported clinical trials and become proactive in developing links with other European MPN groups to become more visible in advocating on behalf of MPN patients.

MPN Voice offers a unique peer support or buddy system, supported by healthcare professionals, putting MPN patients in contact with other patients who can provide a sympathetic and supportive ear for when things are new, tough or confusing.

What are Myeloproliferative Neoplasms (MPNs)?

MPNs are diseases that affect how blood cells are produced in our bodies. Our bodies normally produce billions of blood cells every day. This process occurs in the soft, fatty tissue inside your bones called bone marrow. The bone marrow contains stem cells which grow and mature into all the blood cells that our bodies need like red blood cells, white blood cells and platelets. Each one of these types of cells has a specific job to do inside our bodies.

When a person is diagnosed with an MPN something has gone wrong with their blood cell production. The bone marrow begins to produce either too many blood cells, or sometimes too few. There are three common types of MPNs, but there are other types as well.

The three most common types of MPNs are separated into different disorders as each of them affect blood cell levels in a different way.

- Essential Thrombocythaemia (ET)
- Polycythaemia Vera (PV)
- Myelofibrosis (MF)

Symptoms to watch out for
Itching, night sweats, fever, abdominal pain, feeling full quickly after eating (early satiety), weight loss, bone pain, fatigue, difficulty concentrating and inactivity. A simple ten-point assessment tool, called MPN10, is available to keep track of your symptoms. Ask your haematologist for a copy or use the online version via the MPN Voice website.

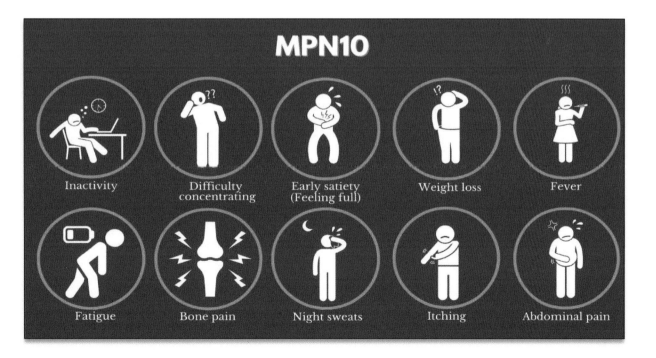

Essential Thrombocythaemia

In ET, the bone marrow makes more platelets than the body needs. Platelets are needed to help blood clot, but in people with ET, overproduction means they don't work properly. This excess of platelets may cause blood clots (thrombosis) which could block a vein or an artery and stop blood flowing or it may cause excess bleeding.

The most common complications are blood clots in the:
- Arteries (arterial thrombosis which may lead to heart attacks, strokes or damage of intestinal tissue, such as gangrene)
- Veins (venous thrombosis including, for example, deep vein thrombosis (DVT) or pulmonary embolism (PE)

Polycythaemia Vera

In PV, the bone marrow makes too many red blood cells (although white blood cell and platelet counts can also be increased), making the blood thicker than normal. In 30% of patients with PV, this excess of red blood cells may cause blood clots to form more easily. Clots can block blood flow through your arteries and veins, leading to the common complications as for ET.

Myelofibrosis

In MF, abnormal stem cells take over the bone marrow leading to fibrosis (scarring) and chronic inflammation. The spleen and then the liver try to compensate by producing red blood cells and this causes the spleen to become enlarged. The consequence is that the marrow is not able to make enough normal blood cells. Patients with ET and PV can go on to develop MF after many years.

Due to the inability of the bone marrow to make enough blood cells, MF patients often have low numbers of red blood cells, white blood cells and/or platelets, resulting in anaemia, neutropenia and thrombocytopenia respectively. All MPN can evolve into a form of acute leukaemia.

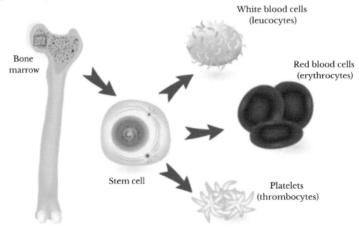

Looking After Yourself

If you suffer from an MPN, it's important to focus on more than just your MPN. MPNs make your blood "sticky," affecting blood flow. This can put you at a higher risk of thrombotic events such as deep vein thrombosis (DVT), heart attack and stroke. It's imperative to do everything in your power to reduce your chances of developing preventable illnesses.

Smoking

Smoking damages your heart and your blood circulation; therefore, it goes without saying, if you smoke then you need to stop! If you need help then ask your doctor or visit www.nhs.uk/better-health/quit-smoking.

Lose weight if necessary

You can reduce the risk of clots by keeping your weight to a normal level. Detailed and reliable information on losing weight is available from the NHS website. Just search "NHS lose weight" to find out more.

Exercise regularly

We all know that exercise lowers the risk of heart disease, strokes, deep vein thrombosis and diabetes in healthy patients. What's more, a study by Harvard University found that daily exercise can help patients reduce their feelings of fatigue.

Review your family history

If some family members have a history of heart disease, diabetes, or breast or colon cancer, you may need more information on preventing these diseases. Additional illnesses such as diabetes can make complications more likely if you also have an MPN.

Get enough sleep

Sleep can be difficult when we are anxious or worried, or busy for that matter, yet it's vital for health. Sleep allows our immune system to function correctly and helps us cope with daily stresses.

Have regular health-screening tests

Basic tests to have from age 40 include checking your weight, blood pressure, cholesterol and fasting blood sugar. Other essential tests are mammograms, cervical cancer tests (Pap tests) and prostate cancer screening.

Control stress

Identify what in your life may be putting you under excessive pressure. Make choices about your activities and workload based on your priorities. Try to focus on what you can control, for instance getting more information and help if you need it. Problem solving techniques can also reduce stress. Search "NHS - Get help with stress" and visit the stress management pages on the MPN Voice website.

Be your own advocate

Read your blood test results in detail. If you feel something is wrong, make sure your doctor understands your concern that something significant has changed.

Staying Active

People with MPNs may feel that exercise and staying active is the last thing that they want to do, especially with the extreme fatigue reported by up to 80% of MPN patients. However medical carers in this field have observed that staying active keeps you mobile, improves circulation and reduces fatigue. Here are some recommendations contributed by Ruben Mesa MD who is Director of UT Health San Antonio MD Anderson Cancer Center and is Mays Family Foundation Distinguished University Presidential Chair Professor of Medicine.

Physicians don't always appreciate just how fatigued MPN patients can feel and often overlook or undervalue the symptoms that MPN patients report. Professor Mesa suggests the following approach:

Define your goals
Writing down your objectives will build your motivation. Your goals can include improving muscle tone, sleeping better and feeling less fatigue. It's useful to define a specific goal that you can measure, such as walking to the bottom of the garden every day or running a 10k race.

Ramp up slowly
The classic error in any exercise programme is doing too much too soon. You will need to increase activity very slowly over time to avoid exhausting or injuring yourself.

Team up with your GP
You should develop a reasonable and modest plan with your GP, considering any limiting factors such as a history of clots. MPN medications are not a major hurdle to physical activity but do check with your health care team before you begin.

Gather your tools
New tools can help you get started. Use a pedometer/smart watch to record the number of steps you walk each day. Keep track of your progress in a logbook. Invest in a comfortable pair of walking shoes and comfy, loose-fitting exercise clothing.

Measure gains over time
You may need to wait many weeks or even months to see an improvement in your energy level and physical condition. That's the case for healthy people and it's equally true for those with MPNs.

Push the limit
The net change over your baseline has the biggest impact. Over time you can push the limit further and further out. Check back with your GP and haematologist and redefine your goals when you feel ready.

Enjoy your new energy
It's clear from the latest research that even a very modest exercise programme can yield tremendous results; you can reduce fatigue, become more mobile, improve circulation and get more oxygen to your tissues. You may never feel quite as good as you did before you had an MPN, but you can feel a whole lot better.

Why is Eating Healthily so Important?

Everyone is aware of the saying 'you are what you eat' and for patients with myeloproliferative neoplasms it is vitally important to pay attention to pursuing as healthy a diet as possible as good nutrition can help to prevent clots.

Why eating healthily is so important
It's true that changing what we eat won't reduce our platelet or red cell counts. But eating healthily is essential for several reasons:

Reduce risks
Maintaining a normal body weight and a healthy body composition can reduce the risk of clots in all people, including those with MPNs.

Deliver vital nutrients
Staying lean helps our heart pump blood throughout our bodies and deliver vital nutrients to our tissues.

Prevent double trouble
Good nutrition prevents other diseases that increase the risk of clots, such as atherosclerosis and diabetes. These disorders are double trouble when you have an MPN.

Two kinds of clots
There are two kinds of clots that concern us as MPN patients and as patients we want to reduce the risk of both kinds of clots.

Atherosclerosis a long-term illness that causes our arteries to harden and develop deposits (plaques) that can break off and cause heart attacks and other clots.

Arterial clots include for example heart attacks and strokes. High amounts of body fat (lipids) and high cholesterol contribute to arterial clots.

Venous clots (in the veins) include deep vein thrombosis (DVTs). Venous clots can be related to body weight and activity levels.

Good nutrition prevents problems
Some diseases that are often associated with growing older have nothing to do with MPNs except that they compound the risks we face as people with MPNs. Good nutrition goes a long way toward preventing common diseases that increase our risk of clots, including:

Diabetes is an illness often caused by being overweight, and this condition also increases the risk of clots.

These above disorders prevent blood from reaching vital organs and add to the "blood stickiness" problems that we have as people with MPNs. The good news is that these problems, unlike MPNs, are preventable. For detailed information on good nutrition and how to maintain a healthy weight, please visit the NHS Healthy Living page (UK) or the Mayo Clinic (US).

Diet and Inflammation

Inflammation plays a key role in the pathogenesis of myeloproliferative neoplasms (MPN) and represents an important therapeutic target for managing symptoms. Symptom burden can have a major impact on the quality of life of MPN patients. This impact is under recognized in the literature. As a result, research into the effect of nutrition on symptoms is lacking.

The Mediterranean diet is based on traditional eating habits that people follow in countries bordering the Mediterranean Sea, including Greece, Italy, and Spain. The diet includes plenty of plant-based foods such as fruits, vegetables, nuts, seeds, beans, pulses, wholegrains, and olive oil. It also includes some dairy and lean proteins like chicken, eggs, and fish to be consumed in moderation. Red and processed meats are usually consumed in much smaller amounts. The Mediterranean diet is rich in antioxidants, trace elements, minerals and vitamins which have anti-inflammatory properties and is one of the most studied diets in scientific literature. Available evidence does not support dietary change as a substitute for medication in MPN but you may find these tips helpful in managing your symptoms.

Studies demonstrate the Mediterranean diet is associated with better cardiovascular health outcomes, reducing the risk and management of type 2 diabetes, reducing the risk of some cancers, improving cognitive function and thus quality of life. There has been a lot of interest in the diet's role in reducing inflammation and level of joint pain for those with rheumatoid arthritis.

It is important to translate and adapt findings of dietary patterns from nutrition research into practical guidance that is culturally sensitive and inclusive to each individual. It is especially important for MPN patients to incorporate the anti-inflammatory principles of the diet due to the role this may play in symptom improvement.

The Principles of an Anti-Inflammatory, Balanced Diet

• Maximising intake of plant-based foods such as fruits, vegetables, beans (like black beans, pinto beans, black-eyed peas, red kidney beans), chickpeas and lentils.

• Basing meals on starchy foods like yams, chapatti, noodles, rice, pasta, bread and cassava –being mindful of portion sizes and opting for wholegrain varieties wherever possible.

• Having at least two portions of fish per week (if suitable). One of which is oily like mackerel, herring, salmon, and sardines.

• Using olive, rapeseed, and sunflower oils as main cooking oil in small amounts instead of palm oil and coconut oil.

• Reducing intake of red meat by having at least two to three meat-free days during each week and consuming more plant-based proteins.

• Eating moderate amounts of dairy products or fortified alternatives.

• Limiting intake of beverages, meals and snacks that are high in saturated fat, salt and sugar.

We hope the following recipes inspire you in the kitchen and demonstrate that with a few small changes to your diet you can make a big impact to your quality of life.

This information was kindly submitted by Bilam Patel, an Oncology Dietitian at Guys and St Thomas' NHS Foundation Trust.

An MPN Patient's Diet Story

Louise, diagnosed in 2005 with PV, found that due to a combination of factors she hit a very difficult and low quality of life in 2011. Determined to fight back she underwent radical changes in her diet which have resulted in a return to amazingly better health and vitality.

Louise shares that, 'At the point of deciding to change my diet I was feeling so ghastly. Malaise, headaches, nausea, searing stabbing pains in my legs, constant pins and needles in my feet and hands, tinnitus in my right ear. I felt like committing suicide!' Adding, 'I'm a hardy old boot and not the suicidal type. All this on top of that tedious PV symptom, fatigue.' At such a low point, a friend suggested that Louise tried an elimination diet rather than going back to the GP for yet more drugs for a urinary infection.

Louise continues, 'For six weeks I only ate organic rice, fruit, vegetables, and organic lamb, drinking water and naturally caffeine free tea; (the withdrawal symptoms over four days from caffeine were horrendous!). Within two weeks I was feeling like a new woman. My headaches, nausea and malaise went, the stabbing pains much reduced, and oddly, the MPN fatigue reduced too. Over the following six months I began to introduce other organic foods into my diet and found that I felt better than I had for years, and all the symptoms disappeared, including fatigue.'

For her current regime, Louise says, 'If I can, I avoid all non-organic meat and fish or in the case of fish, I eat varieties line caught in open waters. I never ever eat chicken unless organic and even then, am careful and prefer chicken from a local soil association accredited farm, others make me very unwell. I never touch dairy produce except for the occasional small amount of organic butter. I don't consume alcohol, processed or tinned foods, drinks or caffeine, including decaffeinated products which are chemically treated. I never consume non-organic sugar whether white or brown, or rock or table salt, only pure sea salt.

Quite a lot of non-organic vegetables and fruits are OK, but I now avoid non-organic potatoes, onions, peppers, celery, mushrooms, butternut squash and beetroot, and non-organic apples, pears, plums, grapes, strawberries, raspberries and blueberries. Thick skinned fruits are fine although I'm careful with mangoes and watermelons depending on the country of origin. I was amazed to see a lot of the above are listed as to be avoided by the Penny Brohn Cancer Care website, almost two years after I'd come to this conclusion myself. I've never been a great devotee of organic food until now, regarding it as overpriced and unnecessary.

How I've changed my tune!'

Diet and MPNs - A Parent's Foreword

My daughter Alice was diagnosed with an MPN when she was 21. She had suffered from migraines with aura since she was 9 and, thankfully, taking a daily antiplatelet medication for ET helped to keep these terrible migraines at bay. Because of this history, we had always tried to eat healthily as a family, cutting out well known migraine 'trigger' foods, such as cheese or chocolate. But the onset of the Covid-19 pandemic in 2020, and the experience of 'shielding' as a vulnerable MPN patient, led Alice to experience new and debilitating neurological symptoms. It was at this point that we decided to change our diet.

After some reading online, we discovered recent research which suggested a healthy, anti-inflammatory, Mediterranean diet could be very beneficial for MPN patients. This was driven by the pioneering work of Dr Angela Fleischman, an MPN clinician in the States, who has identified key links between inflammation, MPN symptoms, and disease progression. Discovering her early trial data that revealed the positive impact an anti-inflammatory diet could have in symptomatic MPN patients prompted us to review our household food intake.

Overnight, we decided to follow her lead and switch to a Mediterranean-style diet, cutting out meat altogether and eating a plentiful supply of healthy, anti-inflammatory ingredients. Crucially, Alice noticed a positive effect on her symptoms within just a few weeks.

The burning, tingling, and crawling sensations she had been experiencing daily reduced in their severity and on some days, disappeared altogether. She had been taking Amitriptyline for this neuropathy for many months - a wonder drug, which had provided almost instantaneous pain relief - but we had to keep steadily increasing her dosage. The new diet changed that, and we liked to think in terms of it helping the Amitriptyline along. The results confirmed to us the value of this nascent work on chronic inflammation in MPNs and the beneficial effect a small lifestyle change could have.

It was within this context that one evening I suggested the idea of an MPN Voice recipe book to Alice. My thought was that the book would contain recipes submitted by patients in the community. It would be a fundraising initiative for the charity and a 'self-help' resource for patients interested in the relationship between nutrition and MPNs.

It has been fantastic to see this recipe book be produced over the last few months by the volunteers at MPN Voice. I would like to thank each person who took the time to submit a recipe in response to the charity's call out and the team at MPN Voice for bringing this idea to life.

We hope you enjoy leafing through the pages that follow. Each recipe has a personal touch, featuring the name of the person who sent it and occasionally, the story behind it. But these recipes are just a starting point. We hope this book will lead to more conversations about diet and symptoms, and what we can do as patients and family support networks to improve the lived experience of MPNs.

I'd like to end by wishing you well on your MPN journey and I hope this collection of recipes provides you with culinary inspiration in the kitchen...

———

Pam, mother to Alice who is 27 and has ET

The Recipes

Jonas' Healthy Breakfast

Submitted by
Jonas Vavra

Time required:
10 minutes

Servings: 1

Ingredients

- 1 courgette
- 5 cherry tomatoes
- 3 cup mushrooms
- 1 tbsp sunflower seeds
- Olive oil
- Salt and pepper
- Multi seeded bread

Steps for Cooking

1. Slice and dice courgette, cherry tomatoes, mushrooms, and fry in a pan with the sunflower seeds until cooked.

2. Add salt and pepper to taste.

3. Serve with multi seeded bread.

Jonas' Notes - I'm a chef, my name is Jonas and I have been diagnosed with Essential Thrombocythaemia, so started to eat more veg.

Franklyn's Breakfast

Submitted by
Franklyn Gellnick

Time required:
15 minutes

Servings: 1

Ingredients

- *4 heaped tbsp Flahavan's Organic Porridge Oats*
- *Alpro 'No Sugars' almond milk*
- *Small handful walnut halves*
- *1-2 tbsp mix of pumpkin, flax, chia and sunflower seeds (I buy individual bags, mix them together and store in a tupperware box)*
- *1 ripe banana*
- *Strawberries*
- *Raspberries*
- *Blackberries*
- *Blueberries*
- *Red seedless grapes*

Steps for Cooking

1. Add the porridge, plant-based milk and finely chopped banana to a saucepan and cook slowly on the hob, stirring occasionally.
2. Wash the desired quantity of berries and put them in a cereal bowl.
3. Break the walnuts into a further cereal bowl and add the seed mix.
4. When the porridge is cooked, add it to the nut/seed bowl and stir well.

Maxine's Hot Baked Nectarines

Submitted by
Maxine Phelan

Time required:
15 minutes

Servings: 1

Ingredients

- *1 tbsp cream cheese*
- *½ tbsp caster sugar*
- *½ tbsp ground almonds*
- *Flaked almonds to decorate*
- *1 nectarine halved and stoned*

Steps for Cooking

1. Put the cream cheese and caster sugar into bowl and cream together until smooth.

2. Work in the ground almonds to make a fairly stiff paste, then stuff both halves of the fruit pressing down the paste into the cavity left by the stone.

3. Arrange the nectarines in a shallow dish. Smooth the surface of each with a fork and sprinkle with flaked almonds.

4. Bake in a pre-heated oven 200C/gas 6 for 6 -10 mins or until fruit is hot and almonds are roasted.

5. Serve with cream or yoghurt.

Maxine's Notes - This recipe is very quick and easy to make and always very popular with our visitors. They are best made in the summer when the nectarines are soft and juicy. If you make too many, they are also just as good cold, which we sometimes have for breakfast, which amuses our friends!

MPN – Martin's Pescatarian Nosh

Submitted by Martin and Susan Fisher

Time required:
30 minutes

Servings: 2

Ingredients

- *Firm white fish (enough for the number of people to serve)*
- *Approx. 1/2 cup lime or lemon juice*
- *Slivers of fresh stem ginger to taste (approx. 1 tbsp per 2 persons)*
- *1 can of coconut cream or coconut milk*
- *Salad ingredients: lettuce, tomatoes, cucumber, red, green & yellow capsicums, onion*
- *Fresh coriander & pine nuts*
- *A loaf of fresh crusty, whole grain bread*
- *Salt & freshly ground black pepper*

Steps for Cooking

1. Cube the fish (off the skin) and marinate together with the salt, pepper, ginger, and enough lime/lemon juice to cover. Leave in fridge overnight.
2. Just before serving, stir in coconut cream (approx. 1/2 can for 2 persons, full for 4 etc.).
3. Serve over a salad of lettuce, tomatoes, cucumber, onion, and a colourful medley of chopped red, green & yellow capsicum sweet peppers.
4. Garnish with fresh coriander leaves and pine nuts.
5. Serve with fresh crusty wholegrain bread (good for mopping the juice).
6. And, for that special occasion, a small glass of your favourite chilled white wine is the perfect match.

Martin's Notes - A few years ago I enjoyed a holiday in Fiji and came across Kokoda: marinated fish. Since being diagnosed with PV, I have been trying to eat more healthily. So, I experimented with the kokoda ingredients (removing the chopped chillies!). We used to call the recipe "Fisher's Fijian Fish Dish" but we thought that the new name would be appropriate for the MPN Voice recipe book!

Diana's Butternut Squash & Spinach Soup

Submitted by
Diana Land

Time required:
30 minutes

Servings: 4

Ingredients

- 1 tbsp olive oil
- 1 onion, sliced
- 1 clove garlic, chopped or crushed
- ¼ tsp chilli flakes
- 1 tsp ground coriander
- 1 medium butternut squash, peeled, seeded and chopped or 400g bag prepared butternut squash
- 140g red lentils, rinsed
- 1 ½ litres vegetable or chicken stock
- 50mls white wine (optional)
- 125g spinach leaves
- Seasoning

Steps for Cooking

1. Sauté onion and garlic gently in oil until soft, do not colour.
2. Add chilli flakes and coriander and cook for 1 minute.
3. Add lentils and squash followed by stock and wine (if used).
4. Simmer for 25 minutes then add spinach until just wilted.
5. Blend.

Diana's Notes - Butternut squashes can be difficult to cut and dangerous perhaps for those of us on a blood thinner. Either use ready prepared squash or put the whole squash in the microwave for 1 ½ -2 mins at high. Let it cool and it is far easier to cut.

Emiliano's Veggie Pasta Bake

Submitted by
Helen Mancini

Time required:
50 minutes

Servings: 2

Ingredients

- 400g tomato passata
- 1 large courgette
- 1 large aubergine
- 1 pepper (red or yellow)
- 10 cherry tomatoes
- Fresh basil leaves
- 1 large yellow onion
- 360g of brown pasta (fusilli)
- 1 fresh mozzarella ball
- Grated parmesan cheese
- 2 garlic cloves
- Extra virgin olive oil
- Salt
- Black pepper

Steps for Cooking

1. In a flat pan, add a little olive oil, when hot add the 2 garlic cloves finely chopped and after 20 seconds add passata. Reduce heat to very low and allow to simmer for 10 minutes.

2. In a second pan, add the olive oil and then add the onion finely chopped and cook for 2 or 3 minutes. Then add the chopped vegetables (courgette, aubergine, pepper).

3. After 10 minutes when the vegetables start to become soft, add the cherry tomatoes cut in half. Add black pepper and a pinch of salt.

4. Pour the vegetables in the pan with the tomato sauce, add the chopped basil leaves, mix all and then turn off the hob.

5. In the meantime, cook the pasta in boiling water for only 5 minutes (it will finish to cook in the oven) and then mix the pasta to the vegetables and the tomato sauce.

6. Using your hands or a knife make small bits of mozzarella and add it to the pasta and vegetables and mix them all.

7. Pour the mix in an ovenproof tray and sprinkle with the grated parmesan cheese.

8. Put in the oven and cook at 180C for 25 minutes.

Helen's Notes - My husband adapted this recipe from his Mamma in Italia using wholemeal pasta and replacing the meat with a cornucopia of delicious vegetables. We often double up so we can reheat for lunch the following day. We hope you enjoy it - buon appetito!

Tamsin's Miso and Peanut Butter Chickpeas

Submitted by
Tamsin Thomas

Time required:
80 minutes

Servings: 6

Ingredients

- 4 large garlic cloves crushed
- 35g fresh ginger grated
- 2 tbsp miso + 1 tsp chilli flakes
- 4 tbsp crunchy peanut butter
- 1 tbsp maple syrup
- 50 ml olive oil + 2 tbsp lime juice
- 1 tbsp cumin seeds
- Salt and black pepper
- 2 400g tins of chickpeas

For the dressing
- 60ml olive oil / 90ml fresh lime juice / 3 tbsp maple syrup
- 1 garlic clove, peeled and crushed

For the salad
- 1 tbsp olive oil
- 150g salted and roasted peanuts
- 200g radishes, thinly sliced
- 1 large cucumber, cut into ½cm-thick slices
- 8 spring onions, thinly sliced on an angle
- 70g fresh coriander leaves

Steps for Cooking

1. Heat the oven to 200C (180C fan)/450F/gas 8.

2. Mix the garlic, ginger, miso, peanut butter, maple syrup, lime juice, olive oil, chilli, cumin seeds and a half-tsp of salt. Add the chickpeas, mix to coat, then spread them out on a greaseproof paper lined oven tray.

3. Roast for 30 to 40 minutes, stirring once halfway, then remove and leave to cool.

4. Mix all the dressing ingredients together with salt and a good grind of pepper.

5. Now the salad - toast the peanuts for 5 mins and don't burn. Once cool, then roughly chop. Roughly chop the coriander.

6. Make the salad by mixing the radishes, cucumber, spring onions and coriander with the dressing, then arrange half this salad on a large plate. Top with half the roasted chickpeas and half the peanuts, then repeat with remaining salad, chickpeas, and peanuts.

7. Serve with wholegrain rice and greens.

8. Any leftovers are delicious served straight from the fridge for lunch the next day.

Tamsin's Notes - I have ET and am always looking out for easy to cook recipes. This one was inspired by Yotam Ottolenghi's. But I've adapted it and made a few changes to it to suit our family tastes.

Beup's Berry Good Smoothie

Submitted by
Laura Reese

Time required:
7 minutes

Servings: 1

Ingredients

- *½ Cup mix of organic frozen strawberries and blackberries*
- *½ Cup organic unsweetened almond milk*
- *½ Cup filtered water*
- *½ Cup organic low-fat dairy or dairy-free yogurt, or scoop organic protein powder*
- *1 heaped tsp organic strawberry jam for sweetness*
- *1 Shake of organic turmeric*
- *1 Shake of organic pepper*

Steps for Cooking

1. Add the ingredients together and just blend away.

Laura's Notes - My inspiration for this recipe after my ET diagnosis was based on a PubMed article, I posted on MPN Voice. It listed strawberries and blackberries as top foods that inhibit JAK2. After reading many MPN Voice posts on the positive anti-inflammatory effects of turmeric, I started keeping my organic turmeric bottle with my salt and pepper. I add a dash here and there to many recipes. I read online that black pepper, berries, and fats help to increase turmeric's bioavailability.

Louise's Sweet Potato & Carrot Mash

Submitted by
Louise Broughton

Time required:
30 minutes

Servings: 4

Ingredients

- 500g carrots
- 500g sweet potatoes
- 3 garlic cloves
- 1 tsp toasted cumin seeds
- 25g butter

Steps for Cooking

1. Chop carrots and sweet potatoes into chunks.
2. Crush the garlic with the side of a knife. This is your bashed garlic.
3. Put the carrots, sweet potatoes, and garlic in a large pan of salted water, bring to the boil, then cook for 12 mins or until soft.
4. Drain the pan and add cumin seeds, butter, and season to taste.
5. Roughly mash then serve immediately.

Karen's Creamy Mushrooms and Beans on Toast

Submitted by
Karen Kennedy

Time required:
25 minutes

Servings: 2

Ingredients

- 250g mushrooms, sliced
- 2 tbsp olive oil
- 1-2 cloves of chopped garlic, depending on size and taste
- 1 heaped tbsp flour
- 250ml unsweetened soya milk
- Half a 400g tin of cannellini beans
- 1tsp wholegrain Dijon mustard
- 2 heaped tbsp finely chopped parsley
- Squeeze of lemon juice
- 2- 4 slices of bread to toast. Ideally ready at the same time, or just before the beans

Steps for Cooking

1. Heat olive oil in a large frying pan. Add mushrooms when hot, allowing them to brown a little before stirring for 1-2 minutes.
2. Turn down heat to low, then add garlic. Cook gently for another couple of minutes.
3. Add flour, and stir round for 1-2 minutes, making sure it doesn't burn.
4. Slowly add the soya milk and stir until sauce is thick and creamy.
5. Add cannellini beans.
6. Season with salt and pepper to taste and the Dijon mustard.
7. Turn off heat, add parsley and a squeeze of lemon juice to taste.
8. Tip onto toast or at the side of toast if you don't like it soggy!

Karen's Notes - It is difficult to tell that the sauce is made from soya milk in this recipe, which was inspired by a Rose Elliot recipe in her classic Complete Vegetarian Cookbook (Cannellini beans with mushrooms and soured cream). With a few tweaks, it has become vegan and lower fat, supporting both our health and the planet. Even my son, a confirmed carnivore, enjoys it. It can also be served with pasta or rice. It is very quick to rustle up for a light lunch, and flavorings can be adapted to taste.

Pam's Courgette and Tomato Sauce for Pasta

Submitted by
Pam

Time required:
25 minutes

Servings: 4

Ingredients

- *1 onion*
- *2 courgettes*
- *500g carton of tomato passata*
- *1 tbsp of olive oil*
- *Sprinkle of mixed herbs*
- *Pepper*

Steps for Cooking

1. Chop onion and slice the courgettes.
2. Heat the olive oil in flat based pan over a medium heat.
3. Add the onion and fry until soft.
4. Add the courgettes and heat for 10 minutes stirring occasionally.
5. Add pepper and mixed herbs to taste.
6. Add carton of tomato passata and simmer on low heat for 15 minutes.

Elizabeth's Garlicky Vegetables

Submitted by
Elizabeth Gross

Time required:
30 minutes

Servings: 4

Ingredients

- *Green beans*
- *Asparagus*
- *Kale or spinach*
- *Broccoli*
- *Optionally, add your favourite veg as required - ideas such as peppers, courgettes, tomatoes etc roast in the same way*

Steps for Cooking

1. It works easily with green beans, asparagus, kale or even spinach.
2. I choose one bundle/clump or handful of the fresh veggie, rinse it off and pat dry with a towel.
3. Heat oven to 350F.
4. Spread veggie on a cookie tray/baking sheet. Drizzle with a bit of olive oil, just a little amount, stir it up/flip them around to coat.
5. Top with a heaped tbsp of garlic (either cut up fresh yourself, or a scoop from jarred garlic in olive oil), spread over veggies. Sprinkle with black pepper and himalayan sea salt.
6. Bake for about 15-20 mins or until lightly bubbling/browned.
7. Enjoy right away, hot.

Elizabeth's Notes - Hi, my name is Elizabeth Gross. I'm a wife and mom and MPN battler. I'm currently 50, and was diagnosed 10 years ago with High Risk, Highly Symptomatic ET pre-MF. A go-to easy recipe we use often is garlicky vegetables they make a great snack, main or side dish.

Christine's Grilled Haloumi and Pepper Salad

Submitted by
Christine Langley

Time required:
30 minutes

Servings: 4

Ingredients

- 4 Romano peppers
- 1 ½ tbsp red wine vinegar
- 75ml plus 50ml extra-virgin olive oil
- 3 cloves garlic, peeled and halved
- Cayenne pepper
- Haloumi cheese (about 255g) (Lighter haloumi can be used)
- Zest of 1 unsprayed lemon and juice of half
- 2 heaped tbsp salted capers, well rinsed
- 16 large basil leaves, sliced
- 110g rocket
- Walnut bread which is good for mopping up any dressing

Steps for Cooking

1. Heat the oven to 190C/375F/gas mark 5.
2. Halve the peppers and remove the seeds. Put them on a baking tray and pour over the red wine vinegar and 75ml of the olive oil.
3. Add the garlic, season with the cayenne pepper and cover with foil. Bake for 10 mins, remove foil and bake for a further 10-15 mins until the peppers are soft.
4. While the peppers are cooking slice the haloumi into eight pieces and set aside. In a large bowl mix together the lemon zest and juice, add the 50ml olive oil, the capers, and the basil.
5. Once cooked, add the peppers and juices to the dressing. Slice the garlic and add to the rest.
6. Heat a grill pan or non-stick frying pan, brush the sliced haloumi with a little oil and griddle it for 2-3 minutes on one side only. Add it to the peppers, toss well and divide the peppers and haloumi onto 4 plates.
7. Toss the rocket in the rest of the dressing and arrange on the side of each plate.

Christine's Notes - This became a family favourite and often came out on a Friday as a good way to welcome the weekend. We have this with walnut bread which is good for mopping up any dressing!

Natalie's Marinated Chicken with Tzatziki Dip and Greek Flatbread

Submitted by
Natalie Mclean

Time required:
30 minutes

Servings: 4

Ingredients

- 4 chicken breasts
- 2 tbsp olive oil
- 1 tbsp oregano
- 1 tsp garlic granules
- 1 tsp parsley
- Half a lemon
- Half a cucumber
- 200g natural yoghurt
- Tbsp mint sauce
- 125g greek yoghurt
- 125g self-rising flour
- 1 red onion
- Handful cherry tomatoes
- 1 cos lettuce
- Feta cheese
- Salt and pepper

Steps for Cooking

1. Marinate 4 chicken breasts in 2 tbsp olive oil, 1 tbsp oregano, 1 tsp garlic granules, 1 tsp parsley, squeeze half a lemon and season with salt and pepper.

2. To make a tzatziki dip, dice cucumber and add to 200g natural yoghurt along with a tbsp of mint sauce, salt and pepper.

3. For the flat breads, combine 125g Greek yoghurt with 125g self-rising flour until the mixture is no longer sticky. Divide in to 4 and roll out into an oval or a round.

4. Slice a red onion, handful of cherry tomatoes and some cos lettuce to be used as a garnish when preparing the flatbreads.

5. Fry the chicken until the juices run clear - add a little more lemon if you feel that the chicken needs more moisture.

6. Heat a dry pan and fry the flat bread until both sides are an even colour. This should take around 2 minutes each side.

7. Load the flat bread with the tzatziki dip, chicken, red onion, tomatoes and lettuce and a sprinkling of feta cheese.

8. The recipe is low in sugar and can easily be made gluten free or dairy free.

Natalie's Notes - I am a MPN patient and think this recipe book is a really good idea! One recipe I always make time and time again is Greek flat breads and the above serves 4 or 2 greedy people like myself hahaha!

Nick's Roasted Mediterranean Salad

Submitted by
Nick Martin

Time required:
60 minutes

Servings: 4

Ingredients

- 1 cucumber
- 750g fresh tomatoes (any size or type)
- 1 large onion
- 1 large red pepper, halved, cored and deseeded and cut into small chunks
- 1 garlic clove, sliced
- 400g tin of borlotti beans, drained and rinsed (or 100g dry borlotti beans, soaked, pressure cooked 35 mins)
- 400g tin black turtle beans, drained and rinsed (or 100g dry black turtle beans, soaked, pressure cooked for 20 mins)
- 50g blanched almonds
- 2 tsp dried oregano
- 2 tbsp extra virgin olive oil
- 1 tbsp red wine vinegar
- 100g pitted olives
- Sea salt
- Black pepper

Steps for Cooking

1. If using dried beans, soak overnight, pressure cook them, and then cool them. Set aside.
2. Preheat the oven to 210C/ 190C fan/ Gas 6 – 7.
3. Cut the cucumber in half, then slice each half lengthways into quarters. Cut each quarter into 2cm chunks and place in a large roasting tin.
4. Cut the tomatoes into bite size chunks. Add to the roasting tin.
5. Add the red pepper.
6. Halve the onion and cut into thin wedges. Slice the garlic thinly. (Slice the chilies if using). Add to the tin.
7. Sprinkle the oregano over, then the olive oil and red wine vinegar. Season with salt and pepper. Mix well.
8. Roast for about 40 minutes until the vegetables are wrinkled and the juices are bubbling.
9. As this is cooking, roast the blanched almonds in a separate dish for a few minutes until beginning to brown.
10. Remove the tray from oven and add the olives, the almonds and the beans. Stir everything together. Return to the oven for a further 10 minutes.

Nick's Notes - This is a family favourite. The aroma from the prepared vegetables fills the kitchen even before cooking begins! I have post ET MF (Jak2+), and a few years ago became unwell, but have been greatly helped by Ruxolitinib. We decided to reassess diet and have been following a Mediterranean style diet very much, on which I feel so much better.

Kathryn's Stuffed Sea Bass

Submitted by Kathryn

Time required:
45 minutes

Servings: 4

Ingredients

- 4 whole sea bass, gutted
- 2 lemons, sliced
- 2 fennel bulbs, sliced
- 2 vine tomatoes, chopped
- 30 kalamata olives, sliced into rings
- 4 garlic cloves, finely chopped
- 300mls dry white wine
- Fresh parsley
- 2 tbsp olive oil
- Garnish of lemon zest

Steps for Cooking

1. Preheat oven to 190C.
2. Line a baking tray with foil, leaving enough spare to form a sealed tent to bake the fish in.
3. Clean the sea bass and pat dry inside then place on the lightly oiled foil to prevent sticking.
4. Stuff the cavity of each sea bass with 2 lemon slices, some fennel slices and some of the chopped tomatoes and sliced olives.
5. Next, decorate the top of the fish with the chopped garlic and the remaining fennel slices and chopped tomatoes and olives.
6. Pour the white wine over and around the fish and season as needed.
7. Drizzle olive oil over the fish and some chopped fresh parsley.
8. Next fold up the foil like a parcel, ensuring it is sealed well.
9. Bake in the oven for 20-25 minutes.
10. Remove from the oven and let it rest for 3-4 minutes.
11. Remove carefully and garnish with lemon zest.
12. Serve with new potatoes and a crisp green salad.

Rosemary's Spicy Lentil Soup

Submitted by
Rosemary Couzens

Time required:
30 minutes

Servings: 2

Ingredients

- *2 oz red lentils*
- *1 onion finely chopped*
- *1 clove garlic crushed*
- *12fl oz + stock of choice*
- *1/2 tsp mild curry powder or paste*

Steps for Cooking

1. Combine all the ingredients together.
2. Bring to the boil in a saucepan and simmer for 25 mins.
3. Remove from heat and blend until smooth.
4. Garnish with twirl of yogurt and coriander leaves if liked.

Lisa's Teriyaki Salmon

Submitted by
Lisa Harrison

Time required:
60 minutes

Servings: 2

Ingredients

- *2 salmon fillets*
- *4-5 tbsp dark soy sauce*
- *1 lime, zest and juice*
- *1 small chilli*
- *2 tbsp maple syrup*
- *1 fat garlic clove, finely chopped*
- *1 chunk of ginger, finely chopped*
- *1 sheet of egg noodles*
- *Bunch of coriander, chopped*
- *1 tbsp sesame oil*
- *Extra lime juice*

Steps for Cooking

1. Heat a pan with a splash of olive oil then fry the ginger, garlic and chopped chilli.

2. Add the zest and juice of the lime and pour in the soy sauce and maple syrup then cook for 1 minute or until reduced and sticky.

3. Pan-fry both pieces of salmon for about 2 minutes each side in a hot pan.

4. The add the salmon to the teriyaki.

5. Cook and drain the noodles, adding the sesame oil, seasoning and coriander and a squeeze of lime. Serve the salmon on a bed of noodles with more chopped coriander.

Dorothy's Tomato and Aubergine Pasta

Submitted by
Dorothy Brown

Time required:
40 minutes

Servings: 4

Ingredients	Steps for Cooking

Ingredients

- 1 aubergine
- 1 onion
- Garlic
- 2 tins chopped tomatoes
- Olive oil
- Pasta
- 1 tbsp balsamic vinegar
- Salt & pepper
- Basil

Steps for Cooking

1. Dice aubergine into 1cm cubes (no need to peel).
2. Sweat in olive oil for 10 to 15 mins.
3. Add chopped onion & garlic and cook until soft.
4. Add 2 tins chopped tomatoes, basil stalks (chopped) and balsamic vinegar.
5. Season and cook for 15 mins (you need quite a bit of salt).
6. Cook pasta.
7. Mix and garnish with basil leaves.
8. Enjoy!

Fiona's Yoghurt Cake with Pistachios

Submitted by
Fiona Mcaine

Time required:
45 minutes

Servings: 6

Ingredients

- *3 separated eggs*
- *70g golden caster sugar*
- *2 vanilla pods, split in half lengthways*
- *350g yoghurt, (I use greek yoghurt)*
- *1 finely grated lemon zest and juice*
- *½ finely grated orange zest*
- *20g plain flour*
- *30g unsalted pistachio nuts, shelled and roughly chopped*

Steps for Cooking

1. Heat the oven to 180C/fan 160C/gas 4 and put a roasting tin half-full of water in to warm on the middle shelf. Have ready a 25 cm round or square baking dish.
2. Beat 3 egg yolks with about 40g of the sugar until thick.
3. Scrape out the seeds from the vanilla pods and mix into the egg and sugar mixture.
4. Add the yoghurt, lemon and orange zests, lemon juice and the flour and mix well.
5. In a separate bowl whisk up the egg whites with the remaining sugar until soft peaks form. Gently and evenly fold the whites into the yoghurt mixture.
6. Pour the mixture into the baking dish.
7. Put the dish in the bain-marie, making sure that the water comes halfway up the tin and cook for about 20 minutes.
8. Then add the chopped pistachios, sprinkling them gently on top and continue cooking for a further 10-15 minutes until the top is light brown in colour.
9. The consistency should be a light sponge on top and a wet custard below. Serve with extra yoghurt.

Fiona's Notes - This Lebanese pudding is delicious warm or chilled and has a very light texture even though it is called a cake. Our neighbours always request this pudding when we get together to socialize as it is so light and delicious. One friend has requested the recipe on a few occasions, but I always decline as I want to keep it to myself. However, if the recipe is published, I will buy him a copy of the MPN recipe book.

Martin's Mediterranean Tuna Pasta

Submitted by Martin

Time required:
35 minutes

Servings: 2

Ingredients

- 1 tbsp of olive oil
- 1 large onion, chopped
- 1 red pepper (optional), chopped
- 2 or 3 garlic cloves, chopped
- 1 400g tin of chopped tomatoes
- 1 260g tin of sweetcorn
- 1 102g of tuna chunks in spring water
- Ground black pepper
- Frozen peas (optional)
- Mixed herbs to taste, that is to say, whatever takes your fancy (basil, rosemary, oregano, parsley).
- The Ready, Steady, Cook professionals always had a bowl of fresh herbs conveniently to hand!

Steps for Cooking

1. Heat a tbsp of olive oil in a deep-frying pan.
2. Add the onion and red pepper (optional) together with the garlic cloves and sweat until soft.
3. Add the tinned tomatoes and simmer on a low heat for 5/10 minutes.
4. Drain the tin of tuna.
5. Add the tuna, sweetcorn and/or frozen peas together with ground black pepper and herbs.
6. Simmer on low heat for a further 10/15 mins whilst cooking a pan of your favourite pasta.
7. Add cooked pasta to the sauce.
8. Serve with a side of fresh vegetables (carrots, cabbage, broccoli, caullflower) or salad.
9. Enjoy!

Martin's Notes - This is my suggestion for the recipe book inspired by my student days guided by Katharine Whitehorn's *Cooking in a Bed Sitter* together with the TV chefs on *Ready, Steady, Cook*. It's quick and easy, nutritious, and very tasty. Ingredients can be doubled up and a portion of the sauce stored in the fridge for later in the week, covered with cling film once cool.

Alice's Lentil and Walnut Pasta Bolognese

Submitted by
Alice

Time required:
60 minutes

Servings: 4-6

Ingredients

- 1 ½ tbsp olive oil
- 1 large onion, chopped
- 4 garlic cloves, chopped
- 1 tsp dried oregano
- 1 tsp dried thyme (or use more oregano)
- 1 ½ tsps salt
- Ground black pepper
- 1 (150g) tube of tomato paste
- 1/2 cup (120 ml) dry red wine (optional)
- 3 cups (720 ml) vegetable broth
- 1 cup (185g) red lentils, soaked for 30-60 mins
- 1/2 cup (64g) walnuts, crushed finely
- 1 (410g) can of crushed tomatoes or whole peeled tomatoes crushed by hand
- 12-16 ounces (340-454g) pasta (such as spaghetti, tagliatelle, penne etc.)
- 1 tbsp balsamic vinegar
- Parsley or basil (optional), chopped

Steps for Cooking

1. Add olive oil to a large pan then heat and add the chopped onion. Add a few spoons of water every few minutes to prevent burning and until the onion is softened and golden brown (10 mins).

2. Add the garlic, thyme, oregano, salt, and pepper. Stir frequently and cook for 1-2 minutes.

3. Stir in the tomato paste and cook for 2-3 minutes until caramelized. Stir frequently and until dark red in colour.

4. If using the red wine, pour into pan and scrape up any browned bits that are stuck to the pan. Cook for 1-2 minutes.

5. Pour in the vegetable broth and stir to combine with the tomato paste. Then add in and stir the lentils and crushed walnuts. Boil, then simmer for 20 minutes.

6. Add in the crushed tomatoes and simmer for another 15-20 minutes until the lentils are tender. Stir occasionally to prevent burning.

7. In the meantime, bring a large pot of water to a boil and add the pasta (of your choosing). Cook until al dente.

8. Taste the Bolognese and add salt and pepper as appropriate. Finish with the balsamic vinegar and stir.

9. Add the cooked pasta to the Bolognese and toss until coated in the sauce and garnish with chopped parsley or basil as you see fit.

Debbie's Courgette and Quinoa Stuffed Peppers

Submitted by
Debbie Street

Time required:
30 minutes

Servings: 4

Ingredients

- *4 peppers – colour of choice*
- *1 courgette, quartered lengthways and thinly sliced*
- *2 250g packs ready-to-eat quinoa*
- *85g feta cheese, finely crumbled*
- *Handful of parsley, roughly chopped*
- *You could substitute ready to eat quinoa with your own prepared quinoa or use your own prepared plain or flavoured rice following the recipe in exactly the same way*

Steps for Cooking

1. Heat oven to 200C/180C fan/gas 6. Cut the peppers in half through the stem and remove the seeds. Place on a baking sheet, drizzle with 1 tbsp olive oil and season well. Roast for 15 mins.

2. Heat 1 tsp of the olive oil in a small pan, add the courgette and cook until soft. Remove from the heat, then stir through the quinoa, feta and parsley. Season with pepper.

3. Divide the quinoa mixture between the pepper halves, then return to the oven for 5 mins to heat through. Serve with a green salad if you like.

Rosie's Mushroom Stroganoff

Submitted by
Rosie Broughton

Time required:
40 minutes

Servings: 4

Ingredients

- 1 tbsp olive oil
- 1 onion, finely diced
- 2 garlic cloves, crushed
- 500g/1lb 2oz mushrooms
- ½ tsp English mustard
- 1 tsp paprika
- 250ml/9fl oz vegetable stock, made from a cube or granules
- 200g/7oz rice
- 200ml/7fl oz soured cream
- 1 lemon, cut into six wedges
- salt and freshly ground black pepper

Steps for Cooking

1. Add oil to a pan and heat. Once hot, add the onion along with a pinch of salt and cook the onion gently for 5–7 minutes or until soft.

2. Add the garlic and cook for 2 minutes, then add the mushrooms. Continue to cook gently for 5–6 minutes, or until the mushrooms are tender and golden brown.

3. Add the mustard and paprika and mix well so that everything is coated. Add the stock, stirring as you pour it. Simmer gently for 5 minutes while you cook the rice.

4. Cook the rice according to the packet instructions.

5. Once the rice is cooked, remove the mushrooms from the heat, stir in the soured cream along with the juice of two lemon wedges and mix it all together. Taste and add salt and pepper as needed.

6. Serve with the rice and the remaining wedges of lemon.

Stacy's Mediterranean Fish Tray Bake

Submitted by
Stacy Suter

Time required:
55 minutes

Servings: 4

Ingredients

- 1 kg baby potatoes (large ones cut in half)
- 500g courgettes – trimmed and chopped
- 1 red onion – cut into wedges
- 1 tbsp olive oil
- 480g salmon fillet – responsibly sourced
- 1 lemon – skin peeled
- 4 sprigs fresh thyme
- 4 sprigs fresh flat parsley
- 2 tins 390g chopped tomatoes
- 100g black olives
- 14g fresh basil

Steps for Cooking

1. Preheat the oven to 200C/gas 6. Add potatoes to a roasting tray and put the courgettes and onion in another Drizzle each with half the olive oil, season and toss to coat. Bake for 30 mins.

2. Meanwhile, make 2-3 slits in the skin of each salmon fillet, then stuff with small pieces of the lemon peel, and the thyme and parsley sprigs.

3. Remove the trays from the oven. Add the potatoes to the courgettes and onion, then pour over the chopped tomatoes and scatter over the olives and half the basil.

4. Top with salmon fillets skin side up. Return to the oven and cook for 10-15 minutes until the salmon is cooked through.

5. Remove from the oven and serve garnished with the remaining basil.

Stacy's Notes – We have been exploring Mediterranean meals after being inspired by an MPN article written about the diet. My partner had only recently been diagnosed with ET Jak2. The article gave us the hope and encouragement we needed to start incorporating the diet into our lives. It has been a blessing in disguise.

My partner was surprised and thrilled that the diet actually includes all of his favourite foods: fish, tomatoes, other various vegetables, and for me I love comfort food, so I am enjoying the pasta, potatoes, and whole foods, it's a win win in our household.

This is our fave dish. We hope you love experimenting with this fab and colourful diet, as it's brought us closer as a couple, we now shop, prep, and dine together, and it's actually brought joy to our lives during this time of uncertainty.

Basil's Gnocchi

Submitted by Basil

Time required:
25 minutes

Servings: 4

Ingredients

- 3 tbsp olive oil
- 2 aubergines cut into 1cm chunks
- 2 garlic cloves, sliced
- 400g can plum tomatoes
- 1 tsp red wine vinegar
- Pinch of chilli flakes (optional)
- Smallish bunch of basil with leaves picked off and stalks finely chopped
- Pinch of sugar
- 500g parmesan or vegetarian alternative to serve
- 700g gnocchi

Steps for Cooking

1. Heat the olive oil in a deep-pan and fry the aubergine with a pinch of salt for about 10 mins or until golden and soft.

2. Add the garlic then fry for 2 mins until smelling fragrant. Add the tomatoes, then half fill the tin with water and add that too. Stir in the vinegar, chilli flakes if using, and basil stalks.

3. Mash the tomatoes to break them up.

4. Simmer for 15 mins until thickened and saucy.

5. Season well, and check for sweetness. Add a pinch of sugar, or a dash more vinegar, if you like.

6. Boil the gnocchi in salted water for 1-2 mins until just starting to float.

7. Drain, keeping some of the starchy water. Add the gnocchi to the sauce with a splash of the water to loosen, if a bit dry, then remove from the heat.

8. Mix the gnocchi into the sauce, then stir in some of the basil. To serve, scatter with more basil and grate over the parmesan.

Richard's Spanish (and a bit of Greek) Chickpea Stew

Submitted by
Richard Ellis

Time required:
60 minutes

Servings: 4

Ingredients

- *2 tomatoes (halved and grated to extract the juice - leaving out the skin)*
- *2 garlic cloves (finely chopped)*
- *1 red or green bell pepper (or even half of each)*
- *1/2 a small butternut squash (diced)*
- *2 sticks celery (finely sliced)*
- *2 carrots (diced)*
- *1 medium red onion, (diced)*
- *1 large potato (cut into chunks about 1/2 an inch thick)*
- *1 tin chickpeas (drained and rinsed)*
- *1 tsp of smoked paprika*
- *1 or 2 bay leaf*
- *Rosemary and thyme - 1/2 tsp each (or to taste)*
- *1 tablespoon fresh parsley*
- *Vegetable stock (preferably a decent quality stock)*
- *Juice of a 1/4 lemon*

Steps for Cooking

To make the thickener:

1. Fry an egg (no runny yoke - pat dry with a kitchen towel after frying to remove the excess oil). Lightly fry bread chunks, in the same pan as used for the egg, or toast until a little crusty. Transfer both to a pestle and mortar, add some fresh parsley and grind until it forms a fine crumb paste.

To make the stew:

2. On medium high heat add a small amount of olive oil, just enough to coat the bottom of the pan. Add the onion and celery. Add garlic. Add pepper.

3. After 5 mins (or once the onion is translucent), add carrots and squash.

4. After 5 mins add in the grated tomatoes. After 2 mins add potatoes and chickpeas, season with salt and pepper, add the paprika, rosemary and thyme. Squeeze in the lemon. Stir gently.

5. Add vegetable broth, to just above the level of the ingredients.

6. Add a bay leaf or two. Simmer on low / medium heat for 20-25 mins.

7. After simmering, add in the thickener. Allow to thicken for about 5 mins. Dress with fresh chopped parsley. (If it hasn't thickened sufficiently, take a ladle full of the juice and veg and blitz. Add the blended veg and juice back to the pan).

Pete's Easy Flexi Stir Fry

Submitted by
Peter Charles

Time required:
25 minutes

Servings: 1

Ingredients

- 1 tbsp of sesame seed oil
- Handful of beansprouts
- ½ handful of fresh egg noodles
- Generous handful of pre prepared stir fry veg
- 4 mushrooms halved or quartered dependent on size
- 6 – 7 cherry or plum tomatoes halved.
- Finely chopped chilli per personal taste
- 2.5cm cubed roughly chopped ginger
- Handful fresh spinach leaves
- 1 sachet of stir fry sauce of choice. We alternate with teriyaki, sweet chilli & garlic, hoisin and garlic
- 75 grams of prawns cooked or raw per preference or availability. Or 75/100 grams cooked chicken. Or any other cooked meat or plant equivalent of choice. Some may prefer to just stick with the stir fry veg

Steps for Cooking

1. Heat the sesame seed oil in a wok.
2. Once hot add in the beansprouts, noodles, stir fry veg, mushroom, tomatoes, chilli and ginger.
3. Stir fry well for 3-4 mins.
4. Add in the sauce of choice and the prawns, cooked meat, or plant equivalent of choice and continue to cook until this is hot. (Slightly longer if raw prawns used to ensure they cooked are through).
5. Add the spinach and cook until wilted.
6. It's ready to serve. You can be creative with any other favourite ingredients you would like to add or those you would like to leave out.

Mark's Paneer and Cashew Curry

Submitted by Mark

Time required:
40 minutes

Servings: 2

Ingredients

- 1 red onion
- 1 red chilli
- 2 tomatoes
- 3 garlic cloves
- 25g cashews (chopped)
- 1 tbsp garam masala
- 6 cardamom pods
- 32g tomato paste
- 15g crispy onions
- 200g paneer
- 130g basmati rice
- Vegetable stock powder

Steps for Cooking

1. Cut paneer into bitesize pieces. Heat a parge pan and add olive oil. Once hot add panner and cook until golden – place to one side.

2. Peel and slice the onion and grate garlic.

3. Add the sliced onion and garlic to the pan and cook for 8 min.

4. Add the basmati rice, cardamom pods and 300ml cold water to a pot with a lid and bring to the boil and cook for 10-15 min.

5. Chop the tomatoes and chilli and boil a kettle.

6. Once the onions have softened, add the garam masala, tomato paste, most of the chopped chilli to the pan then cook for 30 secs. Add the chopped tomatoes and cook for a further 30 secs.

7. Dissolve the vegetable stock mix in 300ml boiled water and add to the pan and cook until the sauce has thickened, and the tomatoes have broken down. Once thickened, add the paneer.

8. Stir the chopped cashews into the curry and cook for 2 min.

9. Serve curry with the cardamom rice, discard the cardamom pods.

10. Enjoy.

Anna's Hoisin Mushrooms and Noodles

Submitted by
Anna Taylor

Time required:
40 minutes

Servings: 2

Ingredients

- 1 red chilli
- 2 garlic cloves
- 2 spring onions
- 150g spring greens
- 40g hoisin sauce
- 15ml soy sauce
- 250g chestnut mushrooms
- 15g root ginger
- 2 wholewheat noodle nests
- 10ml toasted sesame oil

Steps for Cooking

1. Peel and grate the ginger.
2. Cut the chilli in half lengthways, de-seed (scrape the seeds out with a teaspoon) and chop finely.
3. Peel and finely chop (or grate) the garlic.
4. Heat a large pan with a splash of vegetable oil over a medium-high heat. Once hot, crumble in the chestnut mushrooms and cook until they're starting to soften.
5. Add the wholewheat noodles to a pot and bring to the boil, cook until tender, then drain and set aside in a bowl.
6. Pull the leaves off the spring greens, discard the stalks, slice into thin strips. Then slice the spring onions finely.
7. Add the ginger and chopped chilli, hoisin sauce, soy sauce and 50ml cold water to the mushrooms. Season with a pinch of salt and pepper and cook for 5 min.
8. Drizzle olive oil in a hot pan, add the sliced spring greens, chopped garlic and a pinch of salt then cook until starting to wilt. Add a splash of water and cook, covered, for 2 min or until completely wilted, then add in the drained noodles and toasted sesame oil.
9. Serve the mushrooms over the sesame noodles and garnish with the sliced spring onion.

Peer Support: "Buddy" Programme

Do you, a friend or family member have an MPN blood cancer diagnosis? MPN Voice's peer support programme offers individual support to all people with an MPN.

During the course of their disease, people with an MPN such as MF, PV and ET may feel confused, isolated or afraid. Our peer support or "buddy" programme can make a real difference.

Sometimes the best person to speak to is not a relative, partner or friend as initially they may be as confused as you are! Instead, it can help to speak to someone who also has an MPN, a "buddy" or peer group supporter.

The goal of our programme is to help people cope with the physical and emotional side-effects of an MPN blood cancer diagnosis and any difficult feelings related to having a chronic illness.

Your "buddy" can give you support either via email or phone during this often difficult time. They will empathise and perhaps answer questions you might have about everything that comes with having an MPN, as they themselves have already experienced it. This relationship helps both the person offering support and the recipient.

If you need more information, follow MPN Voice on Facebook, Instagram and Twitter or visit our website (search for MPN Voice) for news and updates.

MPN Voice Fundraising

MPN Voice would not exist without fundraising, donations and grants.

The funds we raise enable us to:

- Fund research projects into MPNs and treatment options.
- Funding of website development.
- Provision of printed resources to the healthcare community and patients.
- Providing support to the MPN community via HealthUnlocked, Facebook, Instagram, LinkedIn and Twitter.
- General support to the MPN patient and healthcare communities.

If you would like to know more about how to be involved, simply contact **fundraising@mpnvoice.org.uk** for more details.

LET'S DO THIS TOGETHER

This book will be an integral part of our ongoing fundraising programme. Working with the MPN community for the MPN community is incredibly special and we hope you both enjoy this book and benefit from it, safe in the knowledge you are supporting the continued groundbreaking work that is constantly being done by MPN Voice.

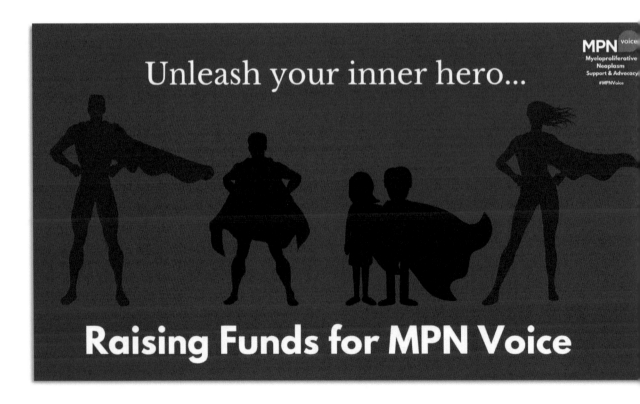

Further Resources on Diet, Inflammation and MPNs

Websites

Diet and MPNs - Alice, Young Patient Blog for MPN Voice:
www.mpnvoice.org.uk/about-us/young-people-and-mpns-blog/diet-and-mpns/
Eating well – MPN Voice:
www.mpnvoice.org.uk/living-with-mpns/ways-to-feel-better/eating-well/
Is there an MPN diet? With Andrew Schorr and Dr Angela Fleischman for Patient Power:
https://patientpower.info/myeloproliferative-neoplasms/living-with-myeloproliferative-neoplasms/is-there-an-mpn-diet
Can Lifestyle and Diet Affect an MPN Patients Outcome? With Esther Schorr and Dr Angela Fleischman for Patient Power:
https://patientpower.info/myeloproliferative-neoplasms/living-with-myeloproliferative-neoplasms/diet-for-mpns-a-nutritional-study

Videos

Living Well with MPNs. The Power of Diet and Exercise: Advice from MPN Experts. With Dr Ruben Mesa for Patient Empowerment Network in 2017:
https://powerfulpatients.org/2017/11/29/living-well-with-mpns-the-power-of-diet-exercise/
Chronic Inflammation in MPNs with Dr Angela Fleischman. Lecture from the 5th Annual Women and MPN Conference in Boston in 2019:
https://youtu.be/FzyoPAGTu-U
Nutrition and MPNs with Dr Angela Fleischman. Presentation at the MPN Horizons conference in 2020:
https://youtu.be/Z5elWgo88_8
Diet as an approach to reduce inflammation in patients with MPNs. With Dr Angela Fleischman for the Video Journal of Haematological Oncology. Interview from the Texas MPN Workshop in 2021:
https://youtu.be/3YHXxfei3Jo

Books

Calimeris, D. and Cook, L., 2017. The Complete Anti-Inflammatory Diet for Beginners: A No-Stress Meal Plan with Easy Recipes to Heal the Immune System. Emeryville: Rockridge Press.
Rankin, F.K., 2022. The Complete Anti-Inflammatory Diet Cookbook for Beginners: 600 Easy Anti-inflammatory Recipes with 21-Day Meal Plan to Reduce Inflammation. Independent Publisher.

Research Articles

Geyer, H.L., Dueck, A.C., Scherber, R.M., and Mesa, R.A., 2015. Impact of Inflammation on Myeloproliferative Neoplasm Symptom Development. Mediators of Inflammation, pp.1-9.
Mendez Luque, L.F., Blackmon, A.L., Ramanathan, G., Fleischman, A.G., 2019. Key Role of Inflammation in Myeloproliferative Neoplasms: Instigator of Disease Initiation, Progression, and Symptoms. Current Hematologic Malignancy Reports, 14, pp.145-153.
Ramanathan, G., Hoover, B.M., and Fleischman, A.G., 2020. Impact of Host, Lifestyle and Environmental Factors in the Pathogenesis of MPN. Cancers, 12, pp.1-15.
Surapaneni, P. and Scherber, R.M., 2019. Integrative Approaches to Managing Myeloproliferative Neoplasms: The Role of Nutrition, Exercise, and Psychological Interventions. Current Hematologic Malignancy Reports, 14, pp.164-170.

Create Your Own Recipes

Recipe _____

Category : _____

Ingredients

_____   _____
_____   _____
_____   _____
_____   _____
_____   _____
_____   _____
_____   _____

Servings :   Prep Time :

Directions

Recipe

Category :

Ingredients

Servings :   Prep Time :

Directions

Recipe

Category :

Ingredients

_____   _____
_____   _____
_____   _____
_____   _____
_____   _____
_____   _____
_____   _____
_____   _____

Servings :   Prep Time :

Directions

Thank you for your support...

MPN voice

www.mpnvoice.org.uk

Printed in Poland
by Amazon Fulfillment
Poland Sp. z o.o., Wrocław

11552185R00031